J. M. SYNGE

AND THE

IRISH DRAMATIC
MOVEMENT

J. M. SYNGE
(From a photograph by James Paterson R.S.A.)

J. M. SYNGE

AND THE

IRISH DRAMATIC
MOVEMENT

BY

FRANCIS BICKLEY

NEW YORK / RUSSELL & RUSSELL

FIRST PUBLISHED IN 1912 BY
CONSTABLE AND COMPANY, LTD.
REISSUED, 1968, BY RUSSELL & RUSSELL
A DIVISION OF ATHENEUM HOUSE, INC.
BY ARRANGEMENT WITH
CONSTABLE AND COMPANY, LTD., LONDON
L. C. CATALOG CARD NO: 68-25027
PRINTED IN THE UNITED STATES OF AMERICA

CONTENTS

NOTE

In the following pages no attempt is made to give Synge his ultimate place in literary history. Two or three hundred years hence will be time enough to begin to think of doing that. My aim has been to show, roughly, where he stood in relation to his contemporaries and, still more roughly, in the line of English-written drama; and to analyse the qualities which make his work so notable. The pages dealing with the Irish Dramatic Movement are to be regarded as background.

I must express my thanks to Mr. Yeats for his kindness in reading proofs and in giving me some valuable hints; also to Mr. Yeats and Mr. Fisher Unwin for permission to print the poem *To Ireland in the Coming Times.*

J. M. SYNGE AND THE IRISH DRAMATIC MOVEMENT

I

SYNGE'S CAREER

JOHN MILLINGTON SYNGE was born near Dublin in 1871, coming from a family which has long owned land in different parts of Ireland. He died at a private hospital in Dublin, March 24th, 1909. His physical life thus came to an early end. His artistic life, on the other hand—its creative phase at least—was late in beginning. Some four or five years of not exceptionally prolific production were the sum of it.

It was not so much that Synge was abnormally late in finding himself, as that he had the unusual wisdom to bide his time. Thus, although in his travel-sketches and poems he has given us a glimpse of the raw material from which his plays were wrought, he has kept carefully hidden the botchings of his 'prentice years.

With his right material close at hand, he at first deliberately turned his back on it. As a boy he wandered among the Wicklow hills.

> I knew the stars, the flowers, and the birds,
> The grey and wintry sides of many glens,
> And did but half remember human words,
> In converse with the mountains, moors and fens,

he writes. But he entered and graduated at Trinity College, Dublin, a proceeding which, according to patriotic Irishmen, withers art and right feeling at their sources.

Synge, at any rate, after taking his degree, left his native land, and forgot what little Gaelic he had known. The desire of self-expression was already strong in him, but he sought his medium in France, in Germany and in Italy. He sought it also in books. From his poems, which are so intensely personal, one may gather a list of the authors of his predilection: Villon, Petrarch, Ronsard, Rabelais, Nash, Cervantes, Herrick. Characteristically, he was concerned with the ages when the quality of energy was at its height in European literature ; but he was also reading more modern stuff. His *wanderjahre* fell in the 'nineties, the day of symbolism and decadence, though, curiously enough, German rather than French influences are apparent in his fledgling literature.

At this work Mr. William Butler Yeats found him in Paris, in 1897 or thereabouts, living in the state of poverty implied by a top floor in the Latin quarter. Mr. Yeats saw at once that the poems and essays Synge showed him were of no value, merely poor examples of the morbidities of the time, " images reflected from mirror to mirror." " He had wandered," writes the poet in his preface to Synge's *Well of the Saints*, " among people whose life is as picturesque as the middle ages, playing his fiddle to Italian sailors, and listening to stories in Bavarian woods, but life had cast no light into his writings." Now it so happened that in these dying moments of the last century Mr. Yeats was at his grand climacteric. Not only was he, as it befell, *nel mezzo del cammin di nostra vita*, but he was also suffering a reaction against the influences of the day, and seeking

11

simpler modes. He, too, had ventured, none more boldly, into the mysterious caves of symbolism, and had returned from his journey with much garnered wisdom, but with a new love for the sun. So he spoke his mind to his new friend. " Give up Paris," he said, " you will never create anything by reading Racine, and Arthur Symons will always be a better critic of French literature. Go to the Aran Islands. Live there as if you were one of the people themselves ; express a life that has never found expression." Many young Irish writers, have profited by Mr. Yeats' clear-sighted and uncompromising criticism ; but none more so than John Synge.[1]

Not that these European years of Synge's were valueless. Probably no experience

---

[1] *Synge and the Ireland of his Time*, by W. B. Yeats, and *A Note concerning a Walk through Connemara with Him*, by J. B. Yeats. These and Mr. John Masefield's article in the *Contemporary Review* (April, 1911) are the best accounts of Synge the man we are likely to get. His manner, lean grey look, and tuft on nether lip gave him a slightly French look. Neither tall nor short, a thick moustache thwarted the play of the mouth, but the eyes, at once smoky and kindling, gave an impression of "a dark, grave face with a great deal in it." He had no perceptible accent. A looker-on, listening outside the circle, aiming at no brilliance, " his merriest talk was like playing catch with an apple of banter, which one afterwards ate and forgot." The gravity of his gaze was memorable.

is utterly valueless to the artist ; and it may well be that contact with France taught him that clean, disillusioned view of life, which gives his plays their lucid reality. There is a sketch called *Under Ether*, an account of personal experiences, printed among his collected works, which Maupassant might have written. Further, if he had kept quite clear of the influences of the 'nineties, it is possible that he would not have developed to quite so perfect a state his gift of fastidious selection.

But when all is said, the fact that so individual a writer as Synge was so ready to follow the advice of a chance critic, is proof almost positive that he felt he was off his proper track. He can hardly have believed in his own *morbidezza*. Certainly there is no trace of it in his published work.

Synge went to Aran, a group of stony islands at the entrance of Galway Bay. There he lived the peasants' life, learned their language, and discovered his own capabilities. Of these days he has left record in a volume of sketches. *The Aran Islands* is a characteristic book. Although a chapter of autobiography, it has little to say directly of the development of the author's soul. By nature reticent, Synge had the objective and impersonal attitude of the true dramatist. One who knew him has said that in conversation he offered few opinions, talking mainly of people and events. He talked little indeed, preferring to watch and listen. So, though his articles on the Congested Districts show that he had thoughts for Ireland's welfare and desired Home Rule as a step towards a better national life, he was always the dispassionate observer rather than the theorist. He saw life in sharp and vivid detail, and grasped instinctively all that would be useful to the artist in him. *The Aran Islands*, and his other similar articles, are like cases of uncut crystals; beautiful in themselves, but from which will be fashioned jewels still more beautiful.

" On some days," he wrote, in one of his rare personal statements, " I feel this island as a perfect home and resting-place; on other days I feel that I am a waif among the people. I can feel more with them than they can feel with me." This confession is very significant. One cannot see an object if one holds it close to one's eyes. The days of identification gave Synge insight, but for the most part he stood a little aloof, not so far as to lose the details of his vision, but not so near as to blur it. If he had become permanently merged with his surroundings, he might have become a lyric poet, but he would not have written the plays. It may be surmised that some of his poems belong to those days when he felt at home, but that the plays were the works of the " waif," the alien observant. They were not, it seems, written on the islands, but in London and Dublin.

Synge's entry of the theatrical world of Dublin was by no means triumphant. Even the superb *Riders to the Sea* failed at first to attract audiences. *The Shadow of the Glen*, his first play to be acted (October 1903), was received not with indifference, but with hostility. Satires on Irish town life, such as Mr. George Moore's *Bending of the Bough*, could be tolerated, but satire on the Irish peasantry —the time-honoured idol of sentimentalists

—was in no wise to be borne. The favourable comparison between Irish women and the women of England or Scotland in the matter of chastity, was a trump card in the hands of the Nationalists. Here was a writer who seemed to call it in question ; such a thing was impolitic, if no worse. It goes without saying that Synge had no desire to lower his compatriots in the eyes of the world. But if he had only found one unchaste woman in the four provinces and had thought her the right stuff for drama he would have dramatised her ; or if he had found none, he would have invented one had his purpose required it. For he was an artist before he was a Nationalist, and a very long way before. The political question did not exist for the dramatist. But to the majority of Irishmen art still means a political pamphlet.

This prompt enmity to Synge's work persisted. It was manifested against *The Well of the Saints*, first performed in February 1905, and culminated just two years later in the demonstration against *The Playboy of the Western World*, in which a man who is supposed to have killed his father is admired as a hero. The ethics of this play will be briefly discussed anon. According to " The Freeman's Journal " it was " calumny gone raving mad." That active body of extreme Nationalists, Sinn Féin, declared war, and at the second performance there was an organised interruption. A number of men in the pit, some of whom were provided with trumpets, raised such a shindy that the actors were reduced to dumb show. Outside the Abbey Theatre also the police were kept busy, and the press demanded the play's withdrawal. But the players went doggedly through the seven performances billed, and by the end of the week opinion had veered considerably in their favour. Opposition was not at an end, however ; there were demonstrations when the play was produced in London and America, and there were domestic dissensions which resulted in at least one able dramatist's temporary withdrawal from the National Theatre Society.

But the leaders, concerned only for good drama, stood by Synge. The supreme importance of their discovery had at once

dawned on them, and from the opening
of the Abbey Theatre until his death,
Synge was coequal with Mr. Yeats and
Lady Gregory in the responsibility of
choosing the plays to be performed there.

II

SYNGE wrote six plays; one of them left incomplete, two of them very short, none long enough to fill the stage for a London evening. On these he has established a reputation which was high at his death, has grown since, and seems as likely to be permanent as that of any man of his generation. It has been claimed for him that he is the greatest imaginative dramatist who has written English since Shakespeare, or at least since the Puritans closed the theatres in 1642. The claim is not as big as at first sight it looks; and even the conservative will find it hard to gainsay. To some extent, however, its validity depends on what one seeks in the theatre.

Synge himself had very definite views on the drama, and he has stated them with the economy and precision which marks all his writing.

" On the stage one must have reality, and one

19

must have joy ; and that is why the intellectual modern drama has failed, and people have grown sick of the false joy of the musical comedy, that has been given them in place of the rich joy found only in what is superb and wild in reality. In a good play every speech should be as fully flavoured as nut or apple, and such speeches cannot be written by anyone who works among people who have shut their lips on poetry."[1]

" The drama is made serious—in the French sense of the word—not by the degree in which it is taken up with problems that are serious in themselves, but by the degree in which it gives the nourishment, not very easy to define, on which our imaginations live. . . . The drama, like the symphony, does not teach or prove anything. . . . Of the things which nourish the imagination, humour is one of the most needful, and it is dangerous to limit or destroy it."[2]

This last pronouncement was evoked by the reception of *The Playboy of the Western World*. Certain Irish towns were apparently losing their humour. " In the greater part of Ireland, however," he con-

[1] Preface to *The Playboy of the Western World*.
[2] Preface to *The Tinker's Wedding*.

soles himself, " the whole people, from the tinkers to the clergy, have still a life, and view of life, that are rich and genial and humorous." He did not think that these people would mind being laughed at without malice.

Art for Synge was an expression, not of life keyed down to the low pitch convenient for those who live in the narrow streets of civilisation, but of life " superb and wild." He would have approved of George Gissing's definition of art as " The expression, satisfying and abiding, of the zest of life." Gissing's " zest " is Synge's " joy," which is no more confined to comedy than his " seriousness " to tragedy or his " reality " to plays of modern life. They are the qualities which nourish the imagination by giving it food richer than the fare of ordinary experience. He had no sympathy with the drama that is concerned with the problems incidental to modern conditions, and differed from the founders of the Irish theatre in his scant reverence for " Ibsen and the Germans."

One has always imagined Shakespeare

going attentively about Stratford or the streets of London, taking notes here of a striking phrase, there of some trait of character sufficiently vivid or eccentric for the emphatic life of the stage. Mr. Bernard Shaw, in his amusing sketch of *The Dark Lady of the Sonnets*, has shown us his possible method ; but in *The Aran Islands* we have an authentic account of a modern artist doing this very thing, though neither the London of his day, nor even the Stratford-on-Avon, would have filled his notebooks.

For though a certain savour of race-prejudice may be traced in some Irishmen's estimate of the Saxon tongue and of modern English literature, it is very clear that the stuff of drama is not so ready to hand as it was in Shakespeare's time. Otherwise it would certainly be used. The reason for this is at least twofold. In the first place our vitality is lower; we are prone to think about life instead of living it, so that even artists deal with special problems rather than with life as a whole. In the second place, our language has undoubtedly deteriorated from the level of art to the level of journalism. One has only to compare the hastiest letter of the sixteenth or seventeenth century with one of the eighteenth or nineteenth to see this. The Elizabethans, and even Wycherley and Congreve, could use speech which only differed from that of the market-place by being a finer selection ; but in the last two centuries the rift has gradually widened between literature and talk. A poetic language has developed which may be a very fine thing to read, but is of no value whatever for drama, which demands something more beautiful than ordinary speech, but of kindred nature. Consequently all that English dramatic literature has to show for two hundred years is the sentimental comedy of the eighteenth century, the dreary blank-verse efforts of the Victorian poets, and, more lately, the naturalistic sociologists. Only by keeping clear of reality altogether—far clearer than Congreve—have two moderns, Wilde and Shaw—the one developing the comedy of manners, the other inventing the comedy of bad manners—contrived to produce plays which are very delightful, but not, it is to be feared, immortal. It may be urged that English genius has turned from the theatre to other forms of art; that is self-evident, but the turn was made from necessity rather than from choice. When so virile a creator as Browning fails to become a dramatist one suspects the matter rather than the man.

But "in Ireland," once more to quote Synge, "for a few years more, we have a popular imagination that is fiery and magnificent, and tender; so that those of us who wish to write start with a chance that is not given to writers in places where the springtime of local life has been forgotten, and the harvest is a memory only, and the straw has been turned into bricks." He found in the Aran Islands and Connemara and Wicklow a peasantry which was perfect material for drama as he had come to believe it should be written; or rather, acquaintance with the people awakened in him a perception of the sort of material the dramatist must use if his art is to be both human and beautiful.

In this people, as he saw it—and he had

no sentimentality to mar his vision—
the god and the beast were mixed in just
proportions; corresponding to that juxta-
position of exaltation and brutality which
figures in his theory of poetry. Very
significant is his story of the old man who,
in " a freak of earthly humour," told him
what he would have done if, in his youth,
he could have had a girl alone with him in
the beehive dwelling where he and Synge
were sitting; and then, a moment later,
was reciting ancient Irish poetry in a
manner which brought tears into his
companion's eyes. This duality justifies
Synge's making Mary Byrne, the drunken
old reprobate of *The Tinker's Wedding*,
break into such lyric utterance as :

" That's a sweet tongue you have, Sarah
Casey ; but if sleep's a grand thing, it's a grand
thing to be waking up a day the like of this,
when there's a warm sun in it, and a kind
air, and you'll hear the cuckoos singing and
crying out on the top of the hill."

When people found fault with his characters
he quoted a paragraph from an article
of his own on the vagrants of Wicklow.

" In all the circumstances of this tramp
life there is a certain wildness that gives
it romance and a peculiar value for those
who look at life in Ireland with an eye
that is aware of the arts also. In all the
healthy movements of art variations from
the ordinary type of manhood are made
interesting for the ordinary man, and in
this way only the higher arts are universal.
Besides this art, however, founded on the
variations which are a condition and effect
of vigorous life, there is another art—
sometimes confounded with it—founded on
the freak of nature, in itself a mere sign
of atavism or disease. This latter art,
which is occupied with the antics of the
freak, is of interest only to the variations
from ordinary minds, and, for this reason,
is never universal. To be quite plain,
the tramp in real life, Hamlet and Faust
in the arts, are variations, but the maniac
in real life, and Des Esseintes and all his
ugly crew in the arts, are freaks only."
It will be observed that Synge, who is
never abnormal or morbid, has tramps or
tinkers prominent in three of his plays ;
finding them a little richer in life than the

ordinary man, and making them a little richer again than he found them.

As with his characters, so with his plots. That of *The Shadow of the Glen* follows closely a story which he heard in Inishmaan, one of the Aran Islands. An anecdote of a man who killed his father with a spade was the germ of *The Playboy*; another, of a woman who saw her son, long drowned, riding on horseback seawards, must have suggested the climax of *Riders to the Sea*. Again, the story which he heard in Wicklow, of two tinkers who agreed with a priest to marry them for half a sovereign and a tin can, developed into *The Tinker's Wedding*. Each of these incidents, slight as some of them were when told him, has, at the outset, a wilder, livelier tinge than the normal occurrences of daily life as we know it. Played on by his vivid imagination it developed into a richly coloured work of art.

So again with the language of the plays. One has only to read *The Playboy* or *Riders*—or hear them finely declaimed by the Irish actors—to recognise that a stage speech has been created more adequate

in its energy and beauty than anything,
at least, since Lady Wishfort abused her
maid, or Millament dictated terms to
Mirabell. Yet Synge claimed never, or
hardly ever, to have used word or phrase
which he had not heard among the Irish
peasantry. He found the English of these
people, whose proper speech is Gaelic,
a " curiously simple yet dignified language "
spoken with a " delicate exotic intonation
that was full of charm " ; and these qualities of simplicity and dignity, rhythm,
delicacy, and strangeness are the qualities
of his prose.

Nevertheless, he did not accept this
folk-language in the gross. As with his
characters and his situations, he bettered
what was already good by fastidious selection and blending. Here, perhaps, more
than anywhere are visible the effects of
his training in Paris, his knowledge of
elaborate literature. For all his energy
he was an artist eclectic and austere, and
it was in language that his art was most
triumphant. " In a good play," he held,
" every speech should be as fully flavoured
as a nut or apple." But in careless converse

many words—though fewer in Inishmaan than in London—must always run to waste. The borders of the finest unpremeditated speech must be trimmed before it is suited for the shapely life of the stage. There is one very interesting instance of how Synge used his material. An old man said to him :

" Listen to what I'm telling you : a man who is not married is no better than an old jackass. He goes into his sister's house, and into his brother's house; he eats a bit in this place and a bit in another place, but he has no home for himself ; like an old jackass straying on the rocks."

This is vivid enough, but in *The Playboy of the Western World* it becomes :

" What's a single man, I ask you, eating a bit in one house and drinking a sup in another, like an old braying jackass strayed upon the rocks ? "

The somewhat rambling original is pruned down to its essentials without sacrifice of any of its picturesqueness. Synge, having discarded the mechanical aid of blank verse, was entirely dependent on his own sense of form for his effects. His art was literally a criticism, a choosing.

Character, situation and language he thus borrowed from actual life, improving and embellishing them, but never altering their essence. His plays are never symbolical, his characters never projections of his own moods and ideas, as with Maeterlinck or Mr. Yeats. But, when all is said, no sincere artist has ever produced absolutely impersonal work. He depicts things as he sees them, and each has his peculiar mental vision. So Synge's work, though objective in method, is subjective in so far as it is coloured by his own temperament. The plays are bound together, and separated from all others, by something less material than their distinctive language ; they are the work, not only of one hand, but of one soul. The moods of his various plays—laughter and passion and knavery—were what he saw in the world ; but the light in which he saw them was his own, a clear hard light, shining neither through rosy nor through smoky glass. If there be an actual reality in things

—an authentic value to stultify all our illusions—Synge was one of the few who have got very near to seeing it. For that reason sentimentalists considered him a cynic.

III

THE Shadow of the Glen, which offended serious-minded Nationalists because it portrayed an Irishwoman a little light in her loving, seems to have been the first finished as well as the first performed of Synge's plays. Founded on an Aran story, its scene is set in Wicklow, which recalls the author's remark that in parts of Wicklow the language was " in some ways more Elizabethan than the English of Connaught, where Irish was used till a much later time." One does not imagine that Synge was guilty of a pedantic scrupulosity in this coincidence, but he certainly located his plays in the east as often as in the west.

Be that as it may, there is no poverty of language in *In the Shadow of the Glen*. Besides the indecorous Nora, the characters are her husband, Dan Burke, who pretends to be dead to test her, a timid young herd, Micheal Dara, of a type which reappears in *The Playboy*, and one of Synge's tramps. The situation is full of grim humour. The ending may be quoted as illustrating all Synge's characteristic virtues.

" *Tramp (at the door).* Come along with me now, lady of the house, and it's not my blather you'll be hearing only, but you'll be hearing the herons crying out over the black lakes, and you'll be hearing the grouse and the owls with them, and the larks and the big thrushes when the days are warm, and it's not from the like of them you'll be hearing a talk of getting old like Peggy Cavanagh, and losing the hair off you, and the light of your eyes, but it's fine songs you'll be hearing when the sun goes up, and there'll be no old fellow wheezing, the like of a sick sheep, close to your ear.

Nora. I'm thinking it's myself will be wheezing that time with lying down under the Heavens when the night is cold ; but you've a fine bit of talk, stranger, and it's with yourself I'll go. (*She goes towards the door, then turns to Dan.*) You think it's a grand thing you're after doing with your letting on to be dead, but what is it at all ? What way would a woman live in a lonesome place the like of this place, and she not making a talk with the men

33

passing? And what way will yourself live from this day, with none to care for you ? What is it you'll have now but a black life, Daniel Burke, and it's not long I'm telling you, till you'll be lying again under that sheet, and you dead surely.

(*She goes out with the Tramp. Micheal is slinking after them, but Dan stops him.*)

Dan. Sit down now and take a little taste of the stuff, Micheal Dara. There's a great drouth on me, and the night is young.

Micheal (*coming back to the table*). And it's very dry I am, surely, with the fear of death you put on me, and I after driving mountain ewes since the turn of the day.

Dan (*throwing away his stick*). I was thinking to strike you, Micheal Dara, but you're a quiet man, God help you, and I don't mind you at all.

(*He pours out two glasses of whisky, and gives one to Micheal.*)

Dan. Your good health, Micheal Dara.

Micheal. God reward you, Daniel Burke, and may you have a long life, and a quiet life, and good health with it.

(*They drink.*)

Riders to the Sea is one of those achievements before which the voice of criticism

SYNGE'S PLAYS

is dumb. Tiny as is its scale, it is as
plainly stamped with greatness as *Hamlet*
or the *Agamemnon*. It is the most imaginative, the most passionate of all Synge's
work, yet as true as any to the life he was
seeking to express. All the terror of life
in the fretted islands, all the mystery and
cruelty of the sea are in it, and the pagan-
ism bred therefrom, the ironic fatalism
which can synthesise the almighty and
most merciful Father with the " blind gods
that cannot spare." " The maternal feeling
is so powerful in these islands that it
gives a life of torment to the women,"
Synge observed ; and " on these islands
the women live only for their children."
This play is his commentary, with the
mother's cry when the last of her six sons
rides down to the waters that have de-
stroyed the rest :

" If it was a hundred horses, or a thousand
horses you had itself, what is the price of a
thousand horses against a son where there is
one son only ? "

And the hardness that must come when
life is at everlasting and hopeless war

with the elements is in the daughter's words :

" It's the life of a young man to be going on the sea, and who would listen to an old woman with one thing and she saying it over ? "

And the bitterness of futile revolt is in the mother's complaint :

" In the big world the old people do be leaving things after them for their sons and children, but in this place it is the young men do be leaving things behind for them that do be old."

But the tragedy of the old woman's revolt is as nothing to the tragedy of her resignation when the tale of her loss is complete :

" They're all gone now, and there isn't anything the sea can do to me. . . . I'll have no call now to be up crying and praying when the wind breaks from the south, and you can hear the surf is in the east, and the surf is in the west, making a great stir with the two noises, and they hitting one on the other. I'll have no call now to be going down and getting Holy Water in the dark nights after Samhain, and I won't care what way the sea is when the other women will be keening."

Beside this, most poetry about the sea is empty rhetoric.

The Tinker's Wedding, though the last play to be published in Synge's lifetime, was actually begun before either *The Shadow of the Glen* or *Riders to the Sea*. It was, however, rewritten before publication. Its contrast with *Riders to the Sea* is complete. It is the lightest-hearted of all Synge's plays, the joyous story of how three tinkers outwitted a priest. The mixture of the sordid and the imaginative, especially manifest in the character of old Mary Byrne, gives the dominant flavour, both here and in *The Well of the Saints*.

The last-named play is unique among Synge's work, in that it has a supernatural element. Partly, perhaps, for this reason, but mainly from some less tangible defect, it is not so interesting as any of the others. Two blind beggars, old and ugly, man and wife, have been told by their neighbours that they are the most beautiful woman, the handsomest man, to be seen thereabouts. A saint restores their sight with holy water, but their gratitude is turned to rage when they learn their real

condition. In the end their blindness
returns, but their illusion is gone for ever.
Synge's laughter is nowhere more bitter
than in this play, and his language lacks
none of its wonted richness. But, for one
reason or another, the imagination is less
fully fed than usual ; the feast of reality
and joy is served in a measure which
(lavish enough for most) is for Synge
comparatively niggard.

The motive of *The Well of the Saints*,
the Irish preference for the dream before
the reality, is also the motive of the much-
discussed *Playboy of the Western World*.
The audience was angry, among other
reasons, because it thought Synge implied
that the peasantry of Mayo considered it
a heroic act to kill one's father. As a
matter of fact he did nothing of the sort.
Politics had blinded its victims to psycho-
logy as well as to art.

Christy Mahon comes into Michael
James's shebeen a stranger and a fugitive.
This is quite enough to stir the interest
of imaginative folk. Flattered by curiosity,
Christy gradually unfolds his tale. A
braggart and a coward, but gifted with

words, he casts a glamour over the sordid business, which, in Pegeen's eyes, is heightened by contrast with the cautious propriety of her cousin and destined husband. The scheming of the detestable widow Quin to get Christy away from the shebeen makes the girl ready to go any lengths to keep him. With every telling of his tale some heroic detail is added, and his success in the sports brings him to the crest of the wave. This is a perfectly natural development, and implies nothing more criminal than a bias towards romance. But when Christy's father makes his appearance, and the boy, to justify himself, is goaded into attempting, before the eyes of his admirers, the deed which he has boasted to have done so well, the scales fall from the eyes of the cheated peasants, and they are zealously bent on retribution. So it seems that, after all, they are as sound morally as æsthetically.

Though not so perfect as the two short plays with which Synge entered literature, *The Playboy* is the fullest and most elaborate of all his works. The situation is more complex, the character-drawing more

detailed, than any he had yet attempted.
It is to this play that the epithet Elizabethan can most aptly be applied. It is a
little world of vigorously painted men and
women, in whose doings and sayings
tragedy and comedy are present in equal
and inextricable measure. Its language
is rich with humour and beauty. The only
fault is that the last act moves a little too
slowly; but this defect is small in comparison with the pleasure that the whole
affords.

During his last illness, Synge was at
work on a play of a different order. This
contemner of queens, as he showed himself
in his poems, was busy in dramatising the
story of Deirdre and the sons of Usna.
He did not have time to perfect this play.
But it was his wont to write several
versions of his plays, and one version of
Deirdre of the Sorrows was found to be
in a fit state for performance and publication.

Synge was not the first among the modern
Irish writers to make Deirdre the heroine
of a tragedy. Her story, which was one of
the Three Sorrowful Stories of Ireland,

is the most moving and the most popular of all Gaelic legends. Two plays, with her name for title, had already been acted in Dublin. Now the writers of these plays, Mr. Yeats and A. E., have the gift of pure lyric in a greater measure, probably, than any other men of their race now living. Their *Deirdres*, though A. E.'s is in prose, are both very beautiful poems. Each of them, however, when viewed as drama, has the defects of plays written by those who are too much poets. They are better to read than to see on the stage. Mr. Yeats and A. E. had become playwrights mainly because of the needs of the national dramatic movement, and their work in consequence is artistic and sincere, but naturally fails to display the virtues of the born dramatist.

Synge, on the other hand, was a born dramatist, and nothing else. His natural trade was play-writing; and his *Deirdre of the Sorrows*, like all his plays, is at least as vivid on the stage as in the book. It would seem that he used the story not because he wanted to do reverence to a national legend, but because he saw dramatic

possibilities in it ; just as Shakespeare
used the tale of Lear or Macbeth. He had
none of the awe of his material which is
the modern romantic's characteristic attitude. He had, one might almost say, a
contempt for his original. Nevertheless he was more faithful to its spirit
than either Mr. Yeats or A. E., who treated
it with greater reverence. This is not
a paradox. In pagan legends, whether
Irish or otherwise, the romantic element is
always conspicuously absent. Romance
is an aftergrowth. It is the hush in the
voice of the modern world, standing in
worship before antiquity. Tennyson, pour-
ing this bated modern spirit into the
loves of Guinevere and Lancelot, spoiled
the story of all its ancient joy. So Mr.
Yeats and A. E. have given Deirdre a
dreamy modern beauty in place of the
rich vitality which was once hers. But
Synge was one of the few moderns who are
sufficiently vigorous by nature not to
stand at gaze before the vitality of another
age. There is no " Celtic melancholy "
in the early stories of Deirdre ; they are
crudely material. In the Leinster version

Deirdre lives for a year with Conchubor after Naisi's death, and then commits suicide in a very brutal fashion. Synge, indeed, like the others, ignores this, and makes Deirdre's death follow immediately on her lover's ; for the original ending is inartistic, a flagrant anticlimax. But essentially *Deirdre of the Sorrows* is as full of life as any prototype, and that is not because Synge was a careful antiquary, skilled to reproduce spirit as well as letter, but because he was not an antiquary at all. He filled the bones of an old tale with his own spirit. It is only the really vigorous artist, with no reverence whatever for any work but his own, who may thus create afresh what older minds have already created.

Deirdre of the Sorrows is as full of life as *The Playboy of the Western World.* Tragic in the highest sense, it never ceases to be human. " At your age," says Naisi to Lavarcham, " you should know there are nights when a king like Conchubor would spit upon his arm ring, and queens will stick their tongues out at the rising moon." These are strange words for

a hero of romance ; and even though some
homeliness would always be in keeping
with the character of the old woman
Lavarcham, she gets very far from the
grand style when she talks about the High
King being in a blue stew. The sinister
and enigmatic character of Owen, deliberately introduced by Synge for the sake of
contrast and solidity, but not developed
as far as he would have been had Synge
lived, is the most Elizabethan figure in
the plays. He is one of the " variations
from the ordinary type of manhood,"
which his creator saw alike in the tramps
of Irish highways and in Hamlet.

Deirdre herself, though superb when
superbness is apt, is a very human figure.
Her farewell to Alban has the same pathos
as Pegeen Mike's grief for her shattered
illusions.

" Woods of Cuan, woods of Cuan, dear
country of the east ! It's seven years we've
had a life was joy only, and this day we're
going west, this day we're facing death, maybe,
and death should be a poor, untidy thing,
though it's a queen that dies."

Pity shows here, as it rarely shows in

Synge's work ; but it is pity for the woman rather than the queen. " Queens get old, Deirdre," says Owen, " with their white and long arms going from them, and their backs hooping. I tell you it's a poor thing to see a queen's nose reaching down to scrape her chin."

The idea that even Deirdre will grow old is the central idea of the play. Fergus, Conchubor's councillor and Naisi's friend, harps on it, and Naisi himself confesses that he has known the fear that some day he will wake to find Deirdre less lovely. Deirdre overhears this confession, and because of it, and in spite of Naisi's passionate eating of his words, insists that the pleasant life in Alban must end. By this note of mortal frailty, which recurs in the bitterness between Naisi and Deirdre at the very last, this ancient story, which had passed through the rarefying flames of romanticism, regains the vitality which in the beginning had been so great as to keep it alive for centuries.

Yet, when all is said, the play is a tragedy and a poem. Fate broods over it and beauty informs it. Synge's prose, be it

repeated, could either smell of the earth
or reflect the light of the stars. And though
its loftier aspect is shown in each of the
plays, it naturally has the greatest scope
in *Deirdre of the Sorrows*, where, however
modern the spirit, the externals at least are
of an antique beauty. Thus does Pegeen
Mike, in *The Playboy*, order her trousseau :

" Six yards of stuff for to make a yellow
gown. A pair of lace boots with lengthy heels
on them and brassy eyes. A hat is suited for
a wedding-day. A fine tooth comb. To be
sent with three barrels of porter in Jimmy
Farrell's creel cart on the evening of the coming
Fair to Mister Michael James Flaherty. With
the best compliments of this season. Margaret
Flaherty."

Thus speaks Deirdre in her pride :

" I will dress like Emer in Dundealgan, or
Maeve in her house in Connaught. If Conchubor'll make me a queen, I'll have the right
of a queen who is a master, taking her own
choice and making a stir to the edges of the
sea. . . . Lay out your mats and hangings
where I can stand this night and look about
me. Lay out the skins of the rams of Connaught and of the goats of the west. I will not

be a child or plaything; I'll put on my robes that are the richest, for I will not be brought down to Emain as Cuchulain brings his horse to the yoke, or Conall Cearneach puts his shield upon his arm; and maybe from this day I will turn the men of Ireland like a wind blowing on the heath."

The theatre to-day has little to offer that can be compared with Miss Maire O'Neill's utterance of these words.

Nor are the beauties of *Deirdre of the Sorrows* merely picturesque. Notwithstanding the grotesque and homely relief, the play moves steadily upwards to its superb climax in Deirdre's last passion and the sudden coming of grey old age on baffled Conchubor. The final scene shows Synge's greatness as a tragic artist even more eminently than *Riders to the Sea*, because in the later play he has to deal with a greater complexity of emotion.

Thus Synge, having written five plays of modern life, began another of which the story, at least, was very old. The question of what this portended is, unhappily, unanswerable; but it is not perhaps an utterly fruitless field of discussion. One's conjecture depends on one's reading of the dramatist.

The too obvious theory that the transition from *The Playboy* to *Deirdre* marks a definite change in Synge's ideas of his art, is sufficiently discredited by the essential homogeneity of the two plays. On the other hand, it is very probable that he intended permanently to enlarge his field. Rich as was the life which he expressed in the earlier plays, he could scarcely have worked indefinitely over such limited ground. The danger of at last becoming mechanical would have been almost unavoidable. It is likely, therefore, that, unless he had come with his trained vision to see dramatic stuff in the life of cities or of foreign countries, he would have often taken his themes from stories already told. So long as it is good, it is of very little moment where the artist finds his material ; and Synge, one may be sure, would never have used any but the best.[1]

[1] Mr. Yeats tells me that, at the time when he was writing *Deirdre of the Sorrows*, Synge told him that he was sick of the Irish peasant on the stage, and that he was contemplating a play of Dublin slum life.

IV

YEATS AND THE MOVEMENT

GRANTED the meeting with Mr. Yeats, it is not likely that Synge's subsequent work would have been other than it was, even if no Irish dramatic movement had been at the time on foot. Many admirable dramatists have come into being purely on account of the needs of the Irish National Theatre Society and the encouragement it has offered. Synge, on the other hand, having once found that drama was his business and Ireland his quarry, would have worked on without external stimulus. Still, though neither parent nor child of the movement, he became one of its most prominent figures and has left his mark on its development. Moreover, it gave him a stage, adequate interpreters, and an audience, without which things even the finest dramatist is not very much better than " an old braying jackass strayed upon the rocks."

Rightly to appreciate this movement, it is necessary to understand, rather in its organic development than in its individual manifestations, the work of the man who for nearly twenty years has been the dominant figure in Irish letters. It has been shown how a crisis in Mr. Yeats' life, rather than in Synge's own, determined the latter's destiny. So with almost the whole of modern Irish literature, both poetry and drama, its progress is inextricably interwoven with the spiritual progress of William Butler Yeats.

Anthologies of Irish poetry usually start with Goldsmith, who was Irish only by birth and a poet only by eighteenth-century standards. Tom Moore did not add much to his country's glory, though he compiled her history and wrote a couple of lyrics which only make his normal banalities the more intolerable. The nineteenth century saw a vast flood of poetry more remarkable for its political fervour than for its æsthetic excellence. The most renowned of these patriot rhymers were Jeremiah Joseph Callanan (1795–1829), John Banim (1798–1842), James Clarence Mangan (1803–49), Edward Walsh (1805–50), Sir Samuel Ferguson (1810–86), Thomas

Osborne Davis (1814–45), and Sir Charles
Gavan Duffy (1816–1903). Chief of these,
from the point of view of their most ardent
admirers, was Davis. One of the founders
of *The Nation*, heart and soul of the Young
Ireland party, he will always be remembered with Smith O'Brien, Gavan Duffy
and John Mitchel as a heroic figure in one
act of the long struggle for Irish liberty.
There is fine rhetoric as well as fine feeling
in such things as *The Lament for Owen
Roe O'Neill*, but Davis never got so near
to achieving high poetry as did Ferguson
or Mangan. Neither of these latter was as
preoccupied with active politics as Davis,
though Ferguson founded the Protestant
Repeal Association as an ally to Young
Ireland, and wrote a noble and sonorous
lament for the man on whom he looked
as the likeliest saviour of his country.

Oh, brave young men, my love, my pride, my promise,
    'Tis on you my hopes are set,
In manliness, in kindness, in justice,
    To make Erin a nation yet :
Self-respecting, self-relying, self-advancing,
    In union or in severance free and strong—
And if God grant this, then under God, to Thomas Davis
    Let the greater praise belong.

Ferguson's chief work was to make known to Irishmen the heroic legends of their land, and he did this both in collections of stories and in poems that often have a fine barbaric note. He looked no lower than Homer for his model, and he had undoubted epic qualities, though marred, as they too often were, by a lack of self-criticism.

Mangan, who stands with Savage and Poe and Verlaine among the poets of disordered lives, is nowadays generally allowed to be the foremost Irish writer of the old dispensation. Enthusiasts for Irish poetry invariably cite his *Dark Rosaleen*[1] to support their attitude. And though its constant position in the window may lead to suspicion of a lack of goods in the store which is not wholly justified, there is no question that that poem stands foremost of its type. Founded, as was so usual, on a Gaelic original, it is the best manifestation both of the ardent patriot-

[1] Dark Rosaleen is, of course, Ireland ; the Roisin Dubh of Thomas Furlong and Aubrey De Vere. The Rose, being both a mystical emblem and a symbol for Ireland, is a recurring figure in Mr. Yeats' poetry.

ism and of the sadness which characterise
this phase of the national literature.

O my Dark Rosaleen,
   Do not sigh, do not weep !
The priests are on the ocean green,
   They march along the deep.
There's wine from the royal Pope,
   Upon the ocean green ;
And Spanish ale shall give you hope,
   My Dark Rosaleen !
   My own Rosaleen !
Shall glad your heart, shall give you hope,
Shall give you health, and help, and hope,
   My Dark Rosaleen !

Over hills and through dales
   Have I roamed for your sake ;
All yesterday I sailed with sails
   On river and on lake.
The Erne at its highest flood,
   I dashed across unseen,
For there was lightning in my blood,
   My Dark Rosaleen !
   My own Rosaleen !
O ! there was lightning in my blood,
Red lightning lightened through my blood,
   My Dark Rosaleen !

All day long, in unrest,
   To and fro do I move,
The very soul within my breast
   Is wasted for you, love !

J. M. SYNGE

The heart in my bosom faints
  To think of you, my Queen,
My life of life, my saint of saints,
  My Dark Rosaleen !
  My own Rosaleen !
To hear your sweet and sad complaints,
My life, my love, my saint of saints,
  My Dark Rosaleen !

Woe and pain, pain and woe,
  Are my lot, night and noon,
To see your bright face clouded so,
  Like to the mournful moon.
But yet will I rear your throne
  Again in golden sheen ;
'Tis you shall reign, shall reign alone,
  My Dark Rosaleen !
  My own Rosaleen !
'Tis you shall have the golden throne,
'Tis you shall reign, and reign alone,
  My Dark Rosaleen !

Over dews, over sands,
  Will I fly for your weal :
Your holy, delicate white hands
  Shall girdle me with steel.
At home in your emerald bowers,
  From morning's dawn till e'en
You'll pray for me, my flower of flowers,
  My Dark Rosaleen !
  My fond Rosaleen !
You'll think of me through daylight's hours,
My virgin flower, my flower of flowers,
  My Dark Rosaleen !

I could scale the blue air,
  I could plough the high hills,
O, I could kneel all night in prayer,
  To heal your many ills !
And one beamy smile from you
  Would float like light between
My toils and me, my own, my true,
  My Dark Rosaleen !
  My fond Rosaleen !
Would give me life and soul anew,
A second life, a soul anew,
  My Dark Rosaleen !

O ! the Erne shall run red
  With redundance of blood,
The earth shall rock beneath our tread,
  And flames warp hill and wood,
And gun-peal and slogan cry,
  Wake many a glen serene,
Ere you shall fade, ere you shall die,
  My Dark Rosaleen !
  My own Rosaleen !
The judgment hour must first be nigh,
Ere you can fade, ere you can die,
  My Dark Rosaleen !

Although Mangan never rose higher than this, he several times flew very near its level. But he did a large amount of really bad work ; and as for the majority of the men whom love of their country drove to song, their verses were nothing but poor copies of second-rate English or Scots models, such as Scott or Macaulay or Campbell : rhetorical fustian. On the other hand, more authentic poets, such as George Darley, were very little concerned to be national ; while Aubrey De Vere, though a fervent patriot, was first and foremost a devout Catholic. Certain poems of William Allingham's come nearest, in their delicate faery quality, to a distinctively Irish artistic utterance. They are, at any rate, most obviously akin with the work of the modern school.

But none of these men quite answered to Mr. Yeats' idea of what an Irish poet should be. He resolved, therefore, to embody that idea in his own person, and to inspire others with an enthusiasm to do likewise. He wanted Irishmen to use the legendary material which their country offered in such abundance, but at the same time to utter nothing that was not the genuine expression of their own temperaments. To use poetry, as the men of *The Nation* had done, for the enunciation of political opinions, was to degrade it. He thought that the artist's patriotism should be implicit rather than explicit ; that literature should be national, not Nationalist. " We cannot," he wrote, " move [the Irish leisured classes] from an apathy, come from their separation from the land they live in, by writing about politics or about Gaelic, but we may move them by becoming men of letters, and expressing primary emotions and truths in ways appropriate to this country." His first important poem, *The Wanderings of Oisin*, published in 1889, might have been written to support his thesis, were it not that it is too beautiful to have been written for any but its own sake.

It was part of Mr. Yeats' creed that the writer's personal preoccupations should be given full play, otherwise his verse would soon ring false and rhetorical. He trusted to the Irish blood to give that common factor by which the school should be recognisable. His two most distinguished allies, for instance, were both Roman Catholics, and, like Aubrey De Vere, at least as much concerned with their religion as with their country. Katherine Tynan (Mrs. Tynan-Hinkson) has written of both with a Franciscan sweetness and simplicity ; Lionel Johnson with a high and delicate austerity.

The death of Lionel Johnson at the age of thirty-five, in 1902, was a real loss to letters. An exquisite critic, he had maintained that the dactylic and anapæstic measures which the Young Ireland writers had borrowed from the hated Englishman were quite inappropriate to the Celtic genius. His own work is testimony in favour of the graver cadences which he commended. His poetry, bathed in a pure white light, contrasts strikingly with the gorgeous colouring of the only other Catholic poet of recent years who can be compared with him for quality ; that is to say, of Francis Thompson. At its best it takes rank with the religious poetry of the seventeenth century, while Johnson's patriotism had nothing modern in its quiet chivalry.

Both Johnson and Mr. Yeats were members of the Rhymers' Club, the select body of poets which used to meet at the

"Cheshire Cheese" for the interchange of their utterances. Both contributed to that once notorious organ of the literary movement of the 'nineties, the *Savoy*. But Lionel Johnson, as an orthodox Catholic, could hardly follow some of the paths trodden by his curious generation. Mr. Yeats was hampered by no such limitations.

The most potent influences among the young English writers of those days, which already seem so far off, were the French decadents and symbolists : Verlaine, Mallarmé, Maeterlinck and the rest. Mr. Yeats was never attacked by the unpleasant disease sometimes called Verlainitis. He never paid court to the muse of Leicester Square. But symbolism had a strong attraction for him. Naturally inclined towards mysticism, a student of the occultism of the East, he found in French literary symbolism a means of expression for that side of his nature. The blurring of outline, which Mallarmé carried to such extravagant lengths, the correspondence of sounds and ideas which reached its logical and ridiculous conclusion

in Arthur Raimbaud's famous sonnet,
beginning :

A noir, E blanc, I rouge, U vert, O bleu, voyelles,
Je dirai quelque jour vos naissances latentes ;

these tendencies found in Mr. Yeats,
though no blind follower, their ablest
English, or English-writing, exponent, as
Mr. Arthur Symons acknowledged in dedi-
cating to him his book on the Symbolist
Movement. Not only did he employ
symbols in his own work in a manner con-
fusing to the laity, but he also found them
in other men's work. His essay on Shelley's
philosophy is a case in point. As he confesses in a later mood, " I only made my
pleasure in him contented pleasure by
massing in my imagination his recurring
images of towers and rivers, and caves
with fountains in them, and that one star
of his, till his world had grown solid
underfoot and consistent enough for the
soul's habitation." His treatment of
Blake's prophetic books was more justifi-
able, though it aroused the wrath of
Swinburne, who regarded all things
mystical and " Celtic " with the sweeping

prejudice which in him did duty for the sense of criticism. . . . And Mr. Yeats' own poetry became full of roses and flaming wings and hierarchies.

These tendencies, however, are not prominent in his earliest work. The *Poems* of 1895, which comprise all the best verse from the books containing *The Wanderings of Oisin* and *The Countess Cathleen*, are mainly connected with the heroic legends and the popular beliefs of Ireland. Some of the songs have all the beauty, enshrined in far more than the art, of folk-music. Mr. Yeats seemed to have recaptured the pure spirit of song for song's sake which made our seventeenth century melodious. All the great romantic and Victorian poets, except Keats, were preoccupied, even though in their own despite, with some scheme of morality or immorality. The decadents were consciously in revolt against the conventions. Mr. Yeats was just calmly and musically emotional. But in *The Wind among the Reeds* of four years later, while the same virtue still flourishes, the esoteric is so much in evidence, that notes bulking nearly as large as the text are needed for its elucidation.

These poems also have an Irish complexion, but the spirit, at least of some of them, came from the East by way of France. The soul of Mr. Yeats, at a particular stage of its development, is completely expressed; but it is only here and there that the soul of Ireland makes a brief appearance.

This temper made Mr. Yeats very aristocratic and exclusive. Art for him belonged to " a little company of studious persons." " The crowds," he wrote, " may applaud good art for a time, but they will forget it when vulgarity invents some new thing, for the only permanent influence of any art is an influence that flows down gradually and imperceptibly, as if through orders and hierarchies." So he turned further and further from common life, writing :

" The arts are, I believe, about to take upon their shoulders the burdens that have lain upon the shoulders of priests, and to lead us back upon our journey by filling our thoughts with the essences of things, and not with things."

He was a reverent admirer of Villiers

de l'Isle Adam, the arch-symbolist, whose play *Axël* was the *Hernani* of the school; who wrote, " As for living, our servants will do that for us," and supplied Mr. Yeats with a motto for his book of mystical tales, *The Secret Rose*.

But if Mr. Yeats ever, in his quietism, forgot what in a later and rather petulant mood he has called " the seeming needs of my fool-driven land," it was only for a moment. He may have carried his pre-occupations with him ; for to see in the Irish peasant one whose " dream has never been entangled by reality," was to see something very different from what, not only Synge but a whole host of later dramatists has seen. But Mr. Yeats has himself reconciled his mysticism with his patriotism in his verses *To Ireland in the Coming Times*.

> Know that I would accounted be
> True brother of that company,
> Who sang to sweeten Ireland's wrong,
> Ballad and story, rann and song ;
> Nor be I any less of them,
> Because the red-rose-bordered hem
> Of her, whose history began
> Before God made the angelic clan,

J. M. SYNGE

Trails all about the written page ;
For in the world's first blossoming age
The light fall of her flying feet
Made Ireland's heart begin to beat ;
And still the starry candles flare
To help her light foot here and there ;
And still the thoughts of Ireland brood
Upon her holy quietude.

Nor may I less be counted one
With Davis, Mangan, Ferguson,
Because to him, who ponders well,
My rhymes more than their rhyming tell
Of the dim wisdoms old and deep,
That God gives unto man in sleep.
For the elemental beings go
About my table to and fro.
In flood and fire and clay and wind,
They huddle from man's pondering mind ;
Yet he who treads in austere ways
May surely meet their ancient gaze.
Man ever journeys on with them
After the red-rose-bordered hem.
Ah, faeries, dancing under the moon,
A Druid land, a Druid tune !

While still I may, I write for you
The love I lived, the dream I knew.
From our birthday, until we die,
Is but the winking of an eye ;
And we, our singing and our love,
The mariners of night above,
And all the wizard things that go
About my table to and fro,

> Are passing on to where may be,
> In truth's consuming ecstasy,
> No place for love and dream at all ;
> For God goes by with white foot-fall.
> I cast my heart into my rhymes,
> That you, in the dim coming times,
> May know how my heart went with them
> After the red-rose-bordered hem. [1]

Thus are synthesised two passions which might have been very quarrelsome lodgers in one breast. As a matter of fact, at the time of the publication of *The Wind among the Reeds*, Mr. Yeats was nearly at the end of that phase of his life when alchemy and mysticism were its predominant interests. The appearance of that book and the discovery of Synge in Paris cannot have been many months apart, and, as already stated, the elder man was at that time in the throes of reaction. There is a passage in *The Adoration of the Magi*—a short story wherein his interest in alchemy is most fully in evidence—which, with reservations, may be taken to describe his change of attitude.

" I have turned into a pathway which will lead me . . . from the Order of the Alchemical

[1] *Poems.* By W. B. Yeats. (Fisher Unwin, 7s. 6d.).

Rose. I no longer live an elaborate and haughty life, but seek to lose myself among the prayers and sorrows of the multitude."

Moreover, Mr. Yeats was in Paris for the purpose of founding an Irish literary society; and the Irish Literary Theatre, if not already in existence, was very near its birth.

V

MR. YEATS' fine ideal had long been to "spread a tradition of life that makes neither great wealth nor great poverty, that makes the arts a national expression of life, that permits even common men to understand good art and high thinking, and to have the fine manners these things can give." As early as 1892 he started the National Literary Society, hoping that this would eventually lead to the formation of a school of Irish drama. This hope was realised by the formation of the Irish Literary Theatre in 1899.

It is remarkable how dependent on Irishmen, from the Restoration onwards, England has been for her plays, or at any rate for her comedies. Congreve, though she fostered him, Ireland cannot claim ; but Farquhar was Irish, and so were Steele, Sheridan, Goldsmith, Wilde and Shaw ; not to mention such lesser lights as Macklin, Sheridan Knowles and Dion Boucicault.

Yet, a dozen years ago, Ireland had never had a national drama.

The names just cited, and the inability of populous England to match them, were sufficient evidence of an Irish genius for drama which only needed organisation and encouragement. Such organisation and encouragement were offered by Mr. Yeats' venture.

The ideals which Mr. Yeats set out to realise cannot be better stated than by quoting a few passages from his essay on "The Reform of the Theatre," which appeared in the third issue of *Samhain*, the occasional organ of the National Theatre Society. " We have to write or find plays that will make the theatre a place of intellectual excitement. . . . If we are to do this we must learn that beauty and truth are always justified of themselves, and that their creation is a greater service to our country than writing that compromises either in the seeming service of a cause. . . . Such plays will require, both in writers and audiences, a stronger feeling for beautiful and appropriate language than one finds in the ordinary theatre.

. . . One must be able to make a king of faery or an old countryman or a modern lover speak that language which is his and nobody's else's, and speak it with so much of emotional subtlety that the hearer may find it hard to know whether it is the thought or the word that has moved him, or whether these could be separated at all." The presentation of these ideal plays was to be aided by a simplification of acting, scenery and costumes, and especially by a reformation in the art of speaking verse. This last has always been very near Mr. Yeats' heart. He abhors the absurd habit, which obtains in the English theatre, of speaking blank verse as though it were bad prose. But unfortunately he has found few companions in sanity.

Mr. Yeats' partners in the establishment of the Irish Literary Theatre were Lady Gregory and Mr. Edward Martyn. They were soon joined by Mr. George Moore, the novelist, who had a practical knowledge of theatrical matters. Their first performance took place on May 8th, 1899, at the Antient Concert Rooms in Dublin, the bill consisting of *The Countess*

Cathleen, by Yeats, and *The Heather Field,*
by Martyn. Both these plays have a
significant note of symbolism, though
there their resemblance ends. The scene
of *The Countess Cathleen,* which was
written several years earlier, lies in the
Elizabethan or any age. It is fine poetry
and contains some beautiful songs. *The
Heather Field* is modern, but except that
it is concerned with the eternal conflict
between the dream and the business, it
has little in common with the later Irish
products. In both this and the same
author's *Maeve,* played in the following
season, the central figure is troubled by
visions of an unattainable beauty, and
worn out in the end by that and by contact
with the worldlings.

The performances in the Antient Concert
Rooms, though marred by every defect of
staging, were so successful that in the following year the society was offered the use
of the Gaiety Theatre. There was played
Mr. Moore's *Bending of the Bough,* a satire
on Irish municipal life, in which the influence
of Ibsen is strong. Heroic Ireland was
represented by Miss Alice Milligan's *The*

THE IRISH THEATRE

Last Feast of the Fianna. The season of
1901 was mainly remarkable for the production of the first play in Gaelic, *The
Twisting of the Rope,* by Dr. Douglas
Hyde, President of the Gaelic League.
Although the National Theatre Society
does not now produce Gaelic plays, a
movement was started which has helped
the Gaelic League much in their efforts
to restore to Ireland its ancient language.

That year, however, saw the end of
the Irish Literary Theatre as originally
conceived, and the defection of Mr. Martyn
and Mr. Moore. In 1902 a company of
Irish players,[1] under the direction of
Messrs. William and Frank Fay, two of
the finest actors the movement has produced, performed several interesting plays,
including Mr. Yeats' beautiful little *Cathleen
ni Houlihan,* the *Deirdre* of A. E., already
mentioned as being written in the prose of
a poet but without much sense of drama,
and Mr. Fred Ryan's satirical *The Laying
of the Foundations,* which may perhaps
be regarded as the prototype of many

[1] The Irish Literary Theatre had had to put up with
English actors.

71

plays since produced. The two last-named
are the only dramatic writings of their
respective authors.

In March 1903 the Irish National
Theatre Society was founded " to continue
on a more permanent basis the work of
the Irish Literary Theatre." It started
life in Molesworth Hall, Dublin, and among
its earliest productions were the first
plays of Synge, Lady Gregory and Mr.
Padraic Colum. In the following year
Miss A. E. F. Horniman, a splendid friend
to drama, placed the Abbey Theatre at
the society's disposal. That theatre is now
identified with one of the most interesting
movements of recent years. About the
end of 1905 the society became a limited
company. The players, who at first gave
their services, are now paid ; but this
change has brought with it no taint of
commercialism. The acting of Miss Sara
Allgood, Miss Maire O'Neill, Mr. Arthur
Sinclair, and their colleagues, is as certainly
inspired by a love of their art as is the work
of the writers who still find in that work
their only reward.

Such, in brief, is the story of the mechani-

cal development of the Irish Theatre.
Its spiritual history is not so obvious.
Many writers have come into the movement, either to stay or to depart, and each
has had his own methods and point of view.
For one of the most admirable things
about both the poets and the dramatists
of modern Ireland has been their sincerity.
Subject to influences they have certainly
been; the greatest artists are that. But of
slavish imitation there has been remarkably
little. The work of nearly every writer has
a clear character of its own. Still, it is
possible, at any rate among the modern
plays, to trace an organic change.

This may be called, very roughly, the
substitution of the spirit of Synge for the
spirit of Ibsen. Very naturally the men
who started the theatre had him who
single-handed had created a national drama
for Norway constantly in their minds.
The common factor in the work of Mr.
Martyn and Mr. Moore is Ibsen's influence.
This influence was never again to appear
so strongly, though it may still be traced
perhaps in some of those searching criti-
cisms to which later writers (such as Mr.

Padraic Colum in *Thomas Muskerry*) have
subjected their country. But Synge considered Ibsen's " joyless and pallid words "
" as old-fashioned as the pharmacopœia
of Galen." That Synge altered the tone
of the theatre it would be hardy to assert;
but it must be remembered, not only that
he was the strongest man connected with
it, but also that he had a voice in the
selection of plays for performance. At
any rate, that series of plays which might
be described as kitchen drama, and is now
the society's most characteristic feature,
began with *In the Shadow of the Glen*.

These plays, though a problem is often
involved, are mainly interesting, to the
Englishman at least, by the richness and
wit of their dialogue. It is there that the
writers most fully display their individu-
alities. " Lady Gregory," says Mr. Yeats,
" has written of the people of the markets
and villages of the West, and their speech,
though less full of peculiar idiom than that
of Mr. Synge's people, is always that
vivid speech which has been shaped through
some generations of English speaking by
those who still think in Gaelic. Mr.

Colum and Mr. Boyle, on the other hand, write of the countryman or the villager of the East or centre of Ireland, who thinks in English, and the speech of their people shows the influence of the newspaper and the National Schools. The people they write of, too, are not true folk; they are the peasant as he is being transformed by modern life, and for that very reason the man of the towns may find it easier to understand them."

Corrupted or not, the Irish idiom as written by Mr. Colum and Mr. Boyle is an excellent language for the stage; that of Mr. Colum is particularly nervous and terse. The following fragment, taken practically at random from *The Fiddler's House*, gives its quality :

" *Brian.* We didn't finish to-day. I'll come in to-morrow and finish.

Maire. O no, Brian, we won't take another day from you.

Brian. Well, what's a day after all? Many's the day and night I put in thinking on you.

Maire. But did you do what I asked you to do ?

Brian. I did. I made it up with my brother. It was never my way before. What I wanted I took with the strong hand ; or if I mightn't put the strong hand on it, I left it alone.

Maire (*eagerly*). Tell me what your brother said to you.

Brian. When I came up to the door, Hugh came out to meet me. ' What destruction are you bringing me ? ' he said. ' There's my hand,' says I, ' and I take your offer.' "

Mr. Colum is one of the best dramatists the Irish Theatre has produced. His characterisation is very real. Each of his three plays, *The Land, The Fiddler's House,* and *Thomas Muskerry,* is concerned with the conflict between the family and the individual will, but this repeated statement of a problem is not monotonous.

Mr. William Boyle's *Mineral Workers* is one of the most elaborate as well as one of the most interesting plays in the annals of the Abbey Theatre. His *Building Fund* is a clever little comedy. Mr. Boyle left the society after the production of *The Playboy.* But he eventually returned, and his plays are now often performed.

Except Mr. Yeats, no writer has worked

harder in the national cause than Lady
Gregory. She was the first to use the now
familiar dialect. By her renderings of the
great Irish legends of the Red Branch and the
Fianna (*Cuchulain of Muirthemne* and *Gods
and Fighting Men*), she has left no excuse
for that ignorance which so hampered the
writers of romantic plays and made elaborate explanatory notes a necessary feature
of Abbey Theatre programmes. She has
turned certain plays of Molière into the
Irish idiom, and these have been performed
at the theatre. She herself has written
plays founded on national legend and
national history. But her best and most
characteristic are her one-act plays of
modern Irish life. Her little comedies,
usually turning on some absurd mis-
understanding, are written with a wonderful
verbal dexterity. The racy quality of
Hyacinth Halvey and *Spreading the News*
is inimitable. *The Rising of the Moon* is
comedy touched with an exquisite pathos,
while *The Gaol Gate* proves that she has
a sure mastery of poignant tragedy. Her
three-act play, *The Image*, is less satis-
factory ; but *Seven Short Plays* is as good,

in its own way, as anything in modern literature.

Mr. Norreys Connell, Mr. S. L. Robinson, Mr. T. C. Murray and Mr. St. John Ervine are writers who deserve attention. Mr. Rutherford Mayne, whose plays have been produced by the Ulster Literary Theatre, the most important follower of the National Theatre Society, is interesting as an example of the fidelity to locality which many of these dramatists practise. His scenes are always laid in County Down, and his characters speak the Irish of Ulster, which is more like the Scots. *The Troth* is a powerful miniature tragedy of tenant and landlord. Like Lady Gregory, Mr. Mayne does better in one act than in three, and thus bears witness to the wisdom of Mr. Yeats' advice, that writers for the theatre should begin, at all events, with simple situations.

Mr. Bernard Shaw, it may be mentioned by the way, wrote *John Bull's Other Island* expressly for the society, which, however, did not feel itself capable of producing so elaborate a work.

One of the objects of the founders of the

National Theatre Society was to present Irishmen with versions of their heroic legends. A few attempts to do this have already been named: Miss Milligan's *Last Feast of the Fianna;* the *Deirdres;* Lady Gregory's *Dervorgilla.* But it has turned out that nearly all the best talent which has been placed at the society's service has occupied itself with modern themes. So Mr. Yeats, almost alone, has supplied the romantic element.

Long before the first performance in the Antient Concert Rooms Mr. Yeats had been writing plays. *The Countess Cathleen* was published in 1892, *The Land of Heart's Desire* in 1894. When engaged on these, their author no doubt hoped that one day they would be acted in a national theatre. That hope has been fulfilled, and Mr. Yeats, the subjective lyrist, has offered himself for judgment as a dramatist.

Remembering all that Mr. Yeats has done for the theatre, it seems ungracious to insist that the drama is not his proper sphere. Yet, as he admits, friends as well as critics have urged the point, regretting that he should neglect his gift of beautiful

lyric utterance. He has answered that
drama has been to him " the search for
more of manful energy, more of cheerful
acceptance of the logic of events, and for
clear outline, instead of those outlines of
lyric poetry that are blurred with desire
and vague regrets." And certainly his
practical interest in the theatre has wrought
a change in his attitude towards life and
art. He has come out of his old brooding
and developed his humanity.

In *Samhain*, and in the book of essays
called *Discoveries* (1907), he has expounded
his new philosophy. He who once wished
to " cast out of serious poetry those ener-
getic rhythms, as of a man running," could
five years later write :

" All good art is extravagant, vehement,
impetuous, shaking the dust of time from its
feet, as it were, and beating against the walls of
the world."

He desires in art " intensity of personal
life, . . . the strength, the essential moment
of a man who would be exciting in the
market or at the dispensary door." Music
does not interest him, being too impersonal,

but he can rejoice in the vitality of a girl playing on a banjo. He is a little bitter about his old desire for impersonal beauty and intellectual essences, and cares to ascend out of common interests " only so far as we can carry the normal, passionate, reasoning self, the personality as a whole." He has indeed deserted the Alchemical Rose.

And yet, when one turns to his plays, one finds that he has not quite been able to fulfil his new ideal. He may be no longer the alchemist, but he is still the purest lyrist of his generation. He is as subjective as ever. His plays are but the portioning of his dream among many mouths. He is too impatient of all but essentials to accept those conventions to which every dramatist must submit. His plays are never bad plays, and they are always good to read as poems ; some of them, such as *Deirdre* and *The Shadowy Waters*, being among the most beautiful poetry that he has written. But instead of gaining by actual dramatic presentation, as even the most poetic plays should, they lose a good deal of their beauty. Moments of them come to us

81

urgently, but as poetry rather than as drama, and in spite of the footlights. But since no play either can or should stay always at its highest point, the lower levels lose their poetry among the stage furniture without taking on that likeness of daily life which, in the theatre, keeps us interested in the intervals of emotion. Mr. Yeats' verse plays are lyrics spoiled of half their loveliness by the ugly mechanism of the stage, while his prose plays are pallid for lack of earthly circumstance. It is only in very short plays, such as *Cathleen ni Houlihan*, where the interest has not to be sustained long, that he is really successful.

In an ideal theatre, with an ideal utterance of verse, such as Mr. Yeats and Mr. Gordon Craig have desired, *Deirdre* and *The Shadowy Waters* would also be ideal. But human drama has to be written for human conditions.

Realising the defects of his virtues, Mr. Yeats has continually rewritten his plays, striving for a more compelling vitality; getting, probably, as near as his nature will allow him to the dramatic. To those who have remonstrated he has finely replied :

> The friends that have it I do wrong
> Whenever I remake a song,
> Should know what issue is at stake :
> It is myself that I remake.

That is the word of a man whose work is his personality. Driven before the wind of his own development, he has written as he must. This is no plainer anywhere than in his latest book, which contains a " heroic farce," *The Green Helmet*, and a number of lyrics. *The Green Helmet*, a short piece in one act, has a buoyant vitality and a fine irreverence which must surprise anyone who has been accustomed to think of Mr. Yeats as, say, the writer of *The Shadowy Waters*. It also shows an advance in his sense of drama, and suggests that the future may, after all, stultify the remonstrants even in their own eyes. The lyrics also are of a documentary interest. Some of them have a harshness and deliberate crudity which are the very antitheses of the murmurous melody of his old songs. But they are nevertheless in the logical line of Mr. Yeats' development, and

are obviously the somewhat pungent fruit
of personal experience. Mr. Yeats has had
his share of the disillusion which inevitably
comes to the idealist who handles reality.
He has had to give much time, which
would otherwise have been devoted to
thought and creation, to weary mechanical
details. Doubtless there have been failures
and disappointments. His audiences, preoccupied with politics, have been at least
as alert for an adverse opinion as for
artistic excellence. Not only Synge's plays,
but others, such as Lady Gregory's *Rising
of the Moon* and Mr. Connell's *Piper*, have
been met with antagonism. These things
are apt to turn to bitterness in the sensitive
mind of a poet.

Still, looking back on the whole work
of the last dozen years, Mr. Yeats has little
cause for dissatisfaction. The National
Theatre Society has succeeded beyond
all hope, though by no means beyond desert.
Its founder could still write, as he proudly
wrote five years ago : " We . . . can say,
as the artist can in every other art, ' We
will give you nothing that does not please
ourselves, and if you do not like it, and we

are still confident that it is good, we will set it before you again, and trust to changing taste.' All true arts, as distinguished from their commercial and mechanical imitation, are a festival where it is the fiddler who calls the tune."

VI

THE LYRISTS

AND while the theatre has been establishing itself more and more firmly as a national institution, the lyre has given forth no attenuated music. A mere list of those who have handled it would cover pages. Most of them, indeed, are very minor players. In a school much mere school-work is bound to be done. Yet the quantity of genuine, if not great, poetry, issued in Ireland in recent years, is a tribute to the power of enthusiasm.

This poetry is full of what Synge has called " the pang of emotion one meets everywhere in Ireland—an emotion that is partly local and patriotic, and partly a share of the desolation that is mixed everywhere with the supreme beauty of the world."

Mr. Seumas O'Sullivan, a typical poet of the school, has struck the precise note in the lines :

THE LYRISTS

It is a whisper among the hazel bushes ;
  It is a long, low, whispering voice that fills
With a sad music the bending and swaying rushes,
  It is a heart beat deep in the quiet hills.

This brooding melancholy—which has long been connected with the Celt, and was prominent in the work of " Fiona Macleod " as well as in that of Mr. Yeats and Lionel Johnson—is the predominant mood of such writers as Miss Ella Young, Miss Eva Gore-Booth, Mr. Thomas Keohler and the late Miss Ethna Carbery.

It is present also in the more individual work of A. E. (Mr. George W. Russell). A painter, a delicate critic, with the fine prose style which made his *Deirdre* play good to read, a clear and practical writer on Irish economics, A. E. is a poet who can stand without the support of the brothers and sisters of a movement. He is a mystic, though not of the cabalistic order ; his is the mysticism of the passionate pantheist.

So love, a burning multitude, a seraph wind which
    blows
From out the deep of being to the deep of being
    goes :

And sun and moon and starry fires and earth and air
   and sea
Are creatures from the deep let loose who pause in
   ecstasy ;
Or wing their wild and heavenly way until again they
   find
The ancient deep and fade therein, enraptured, bright
   and blind.

A. E.'s poetry is full of an elusive ecstasy, made the more wraith-like by the subtle cadences of its verse.

Mystics also are Mr. John Eglinton ; Mr. Charles Weekes, whose brief, concentrated poems are the utterances of a sincere and deep intellectual force ; and Miss Susan L. Mitchell.

Typical in their simplicity and their note of faery and dream are the poems of the late Nora Hopper (Mrs. Chesson), who stood at the head of the movement with Mr. Yeats and Lionel Johnson and Mrs. Tynan-Hinkson.

Simplicity, again, is one of the virtues in the dialect poems of " Moira O'Neill," and in the very different work of Mr. Seosamh MacCathmhaoil and Mr. Padraic Colum.   Mr. Colum has got a fine tang of the peat and the keen mountain wind into his *Wild Earth*. His unrhymed poem of *The Plougher* is one of the most distinctive poems lately written. In Mr. MacCathmhaoil's verses simplicity is carried even to nakedness. But they have a magic of their own, and are full both of piety and of patriotism.

It need hardly be said that patriotism is the original motive of most of this modern Irish poetry. Attachment to the very soil of Ireland, or of little Irish places, finds repeated expression, while the devoted Irish dead have many celebrants.

> She moves most sad and beautiful
>   Amid her hills of green ;
> She weeps the brave, the dutiful,
>   Who owned her once for queen.

That is the constant sentiment, not only of Mr. Shane Leslie, who wrote these lines, but of a score of others. Among those who have devoted themselves most explicitly to themes of their country may be mentioned Miss Alice Milligan and Mr. James H. Cousins. Miss Milligan has sung the heroic legends, while Mr. Cousins' verse is permeated with Irish lore. A picturesque version of a famous story is Mr. Herbert Trench's *Deirdre Wed;* but Mr. Trench has made very free with his original and does not in any way belong to the school. Miss Jane Barlow, again, though her themes are mainly Irish, has a strongly individual note, and must be accounted an independent.

But with the exception of the two writers last named, and perhaps of Mr. Charles Weekes, all the poets and poetesses so inadequately characterised in the foregoing pages, however various their quality, belong to the tradition. Consciously or unconsciously, they have all accepted and expressed the idea of the gentle, melancholy, down-trodden Gael, living among past glories and future hopes. And it is noticeable that the most marked individuality is to be found among the older writers, such as A. E. and Miss Barlow. Recently, however, a new voice has been heard. Mr. James Stephens, who, by calling his book *Insurrections*, would seem to hoist a flag, has his own grim and humorous view of life which is far removed from, if not actually hostile to, the Celtic convention. Mr. Stephens' work is already strong. If it grows strong enough to become an influence, it may bring a new element into Irish poetry.

VII

IN his realism Mr. Stephens resembles
Synge, though the two men have little
else in common. But Synge also was in
revolt against the traditions of poetry;
and it is that fact, rather than their intrinsic
value, which gives his verses their interest.
They are the most complete personal
revelations which he has left us, showing
us the man with all his " astringent joy and
hardness."

In the short preface, written three months
before he died for the volume of *Poems and
Translations* which was not issued until
after his death, Synge explained his theory
of poetry. He felt that modern poetry
had got too far away from life, both in its
language and in its material. Men like
Villon and Herrick and Burns had put the
whole of their experience into their verse,
which had consequently appealed to men
and not to cliques. The poetry of exaltation would always be the highest, but

" the strong things of life are needed in poetry also, to show that what is exalted, or tender, is not made by feeble blood. It may almost be said," he concludes, " that before verse can be human again it must learn to be brutal."

His poems, he explains, were for the most part composed before these views were formulated, but they might have been written in their support. The majority of them were, indeed, written towards the end of his life. In a letter to Mr. Yeats, dated September 1908, he says, " You will gather that I am most interested now in my grimmer verses, and the ballads (which are from actual life)." Energy, being a rare quality in modern literature, is usually self-conscious and proclaims its presence on the big drum ; and Synge, though there was so much in him that was genuinely Eliza-bethan, turned a little hectically towards violence as he felt life slipping away. In such poems as *In May*, *A Question*, and the mocking *Curse* on one who disapproved of *The Playboy*, he successfully achieves the brutality of which he speaks ; and only in the first instance without detriment to the poetry.

So, again, against a certain kind of romance he is very violent. *The Passing of the Shee*—" Ye plumed yet skinny Shee " —has often been quoted, and might be profitably compared with Mr. Yeats' *Hosting of the Sidhe* as a study in points of view. In *Queens*, after naming with scant reverence the royal ladies of story, he concludes :

> Yet these are rotten—I ask their pardon—
> And we've the sun on rock and garden,
> These are rotten, so you're the Queen
> Of all are living, or have been.

Such exaltation of the living above the dead is sound philosophy; but, if it had been Synge's from the beginning, it is doubtful whether he would have given it such vehement expression. These poems rather suggest that he, too, had trod the vague paths of dreamland, and was angry with himself for so doing. There is a touch of temper about them, which makes one feel that they were written in reaction rather than in a normal mood. He translated Petrarch into that prose of his which is

so much fuller of beauty than his verse;
but when he translated Villon, he chose the
Complaint of the Fair Armouress with its
implacable realism rather than the *Ballade
of the Ladies of Old Time,* which he doubtless thought fittingly rendered in the
" poetic diction " of Rossetti.

By far the best of his poems are those
connected with the peasant life of the Aran
Islands. They have the same selective
realism as his plays and a purely spon-
taneous vitality. " Reality and joy " are
at their highest in *Beg-Innish,* and some of
his ballads have rarely been surpassed since
ballad-making became an anachronism.
Whatever their limitations, there is always
a good smell of earth about Synge's
verses, and that clarity of atmosphere
which is round all his work and makes him
comparable with no other modern poet
so aptly as with Mr. A. E. Housman, of
The Shropshire Lad.

Still, the most valuable quality of these
poems is that they are the personal confes-
sions of an artist whose real art was objective. They enable us to understand how it

was that Synge was satisfied neither with modern romance, nor with modern symbolism, nor with modern realism, but turned into the path which English literature had left for nearly three hundred years ; leaving which, it had lost its drama.

SOME ESTIMATES OF SYNGE, ETC.

YEATS, W. B. . . Synge and the Ireland of
his Time. 1911.

MASEFIELD, JOHN . John M. Synge.
Contemporary Review, April, 1911.

TENNYSON, CHARLES Irish Plays and Playwrights.
Quarterly Review, July, 1911.

TENNYSON, CHARLES The Rise of the Irish Theatre.
Contemporary Review, August, 1911.

FIGGIS, DARRELL . The Art of J. M. Synge.
Fortnightly Review, December, 1911.

BICKLEY, FRANCIS . Synge and the Drama.
New Quarterly, February, 1910.